Driver & Vehicle
Standards
Agency

DRIVER CPC

the **OFFICIAL DVSA GUIDE** for
Professional Goods Vehicle Drivers

London: TSO

Written and compiled by the Driver and Vehicle Standards Agency Learning Materials department and industry experts.

© Crown copyright 2009

First edition Crown copyright 2009
Fourteenth impression 2018

ISBN 978 0 11 553001 2

A CIP catalogue record for this book is available from the British Library

Other titles in the Driving Skills series

The Official DVSA Guide to Driving – the essential skills
The Official DVSA Guide to Better Driving
The Official DVSA Theory Test for Car Drivers
The Official DVSA Theory Test for Car Drivers (DVD-ROM)
The Official DVSA Guide to Learning to Drive
The Official DVSA Guide to Hazard Perception (DVD-ROM)

The Official DVSA Theory Test Kit iPhone/Android App
The Official DVSA Highway Code iPhone App
The Official DVSA Hazard Perception Practice iOS App

The Official DVSA Guide to Riding – the essential skills
The Official DVSA Theory Test for Motorcyclists
The Official DVSA Theory Test for Motorcyclists (DVD-ROM)
The Official DVSA Guide to Learning to Ride
Better Biking – the official DVSA training aid (DVD)

The Official DVSA Guide to Driving Buses and Coaches
The Official DVSA Guide to Driving Goods Vehicles
The Official DVSA Theory Test for Drivers of Large Vehicles
The Official DVSA Theory Test for Drivers of Large Vehicles (DVD-ROM)
Driver CPC – the official DVSA guide for professional bus and coach drivers

The Official DVSA Guide to Tractor and Specialist Vehicle Driving Tests
The Official DVSA Theory Test for Approved Driving Instructors (DVD-ROM)

Every effort has been made to ensure that the information contained in this publication is accurate at the time of going to press. The Stationery Office cannot be held responsible for any inaccuracies. Information in this book is for guidance only. All metric and imperial conversions in this book are approximate.

Acknowledgements

The Driver and Vehicle Standards Agency (DVSA) would like to thank the staff of the following organisations for their contribution to the production of this publication:

Chris Campbell, Skills for Logistics
Patrick Henry, Kuehne+Nagel
David Jackson, Lancaster Training Services
Lorenzo Milani, Kuehne+Nagel Drinks Logistics
Terry Rose, Denby Transport Ltd
Ruth Wallace, Wallace School of Transport
Steve Williams, Truckuk
Freight Transport Association
Road Haulage Association

We're turning over a new leaf.

RECYCLED
Paper made from
recycled material
FSC® C002151

Find us online

> GOV.UK – Simpler, clearer, faster

GOV.UK is the best place to find government services and information for

- car drivers
- motorcyclists
- driving licences
- driving and riding tests
- towing a caravan or trailer
- medical rules
- driving and riding for a living
- online services.

Visit **www.gov.uk** and try it out.

You can also find contact details for DVSA and other motoring agencies like DVLA at **www.gov.uk**

You'll notice that links to **GOV.UK**, the UK's new central government site, don't always take you to a specific page. This is because this new kind of site constantly adapts to what people really search for and so such static links would quickly go out of date. Try it out. Simply search what you need from your preferred search site or from **www.gov.uk** and you should find what you're looking for. You can give feedback to the Government Digital Service from the website.

Driver & Vehicle Standards Agency

The Driver and Vehicle Standards Agency (DVSA) is an executive agency of the Department for Transport.

We improve road safety in Great Britain by setting standards for driving and motorcycling, and making sure drivers, vehicle operators and MOT garages understand and follow roadworthiness standards. We also provide a range of licensing, testing, education and enforcement services.

www.gov.uk/dvsa

The Driver and Vehicle Agency (DVA) is an executive agency within the Department of the Environment for Northern Ireland.

Its primary aim is to promote and improve road safety through the advancement of driving standards and implementation of the government's policies for improving the mechanical standards of vehicles.

nidirect.gov.uk/motoring

Contents

section **one**
INTRODUCTION

This section covers
- The Driver CPC qualification
- How to get your Driver CPC
- Who needs to obtain Driver CPC?
- What's in the test?

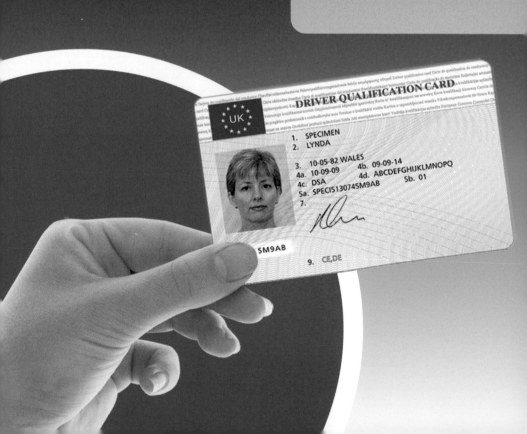

A message from the Chief Driving Examiner

As the driver of a goods vehicle you have a special responsibility – not just to yourself, but to all other road users. A professional driver should set an example to others by ensuring that the vehicle is driven at all times with the utmost safety, and with courtesy and consideration for everyone else on today's busy roads.

The Driver Certificate of Professional Competence (Driver CPC) is a qualification that lorry drivers need to hold in addition to their vocational driving licence if they wish to drive professionally. The aims of Driver CPC are not only to improve the knowledge and skills of goods vehicle drivers before they start work, but also to ensure that these skills are developed throughout their working life. It's also expected to improve road safety by creating better-qualified drivers.

This book is designed to help trainees prepare for the initial qualification tests and to provide a resource that can be used by trainers to assist in developing the knowledge, skills and understanding of drivers. This will enable drivers to adopt a responsible attitude and drive in a safe and fuel-efficient manner.

One of the major challenges faced by drivers of large vehicles is to safely navigate urban environments without putting vulnerable road users, such as cyclists, at risk. I strongly encourage all professional drivers to consider undertaking periodic training on subjects such as vulnerable road users or safe urban driving.

Training and adequate preparation will help lay the foundations necessary to become a safe professional driver for life.

Lesley Young

Chief Driving Examiner

The Driver CPC qualification

Driver CPC was introduced in 2008 for bus and coach drivers, and in 2009 for lorry drivers.

In 2003, the European Union (EU) passed the Driver CPC Directive, which introduced the initial qualification for new drivers. This increases the amount of knowledge that drivers need to acquire before they can drive professionally.

If you're learning to drive a goods vehicle and intend to drive in a professional capacity in the EU, then you'll need Driver CPC in addition to your vocational licence. Bus and coach drivers have their own version of Driver CPC.

The purpose of Driver CPC is to improve the knowledge and skills of lorry (and bus and coach) drivers when they start work, and also to ensure that their skills are developed throughout their working life. Driver CPC is expected to

- improve road safety and reduce casualties by ensuring that drivers are better qualified

- help the road freight and passenger transport industries achieve and maintain better staff performance, better recruitment and staff retention, and more economical vehicle usage

- improve and maintain the skill levels of professional drivers

- mitigate against damage to the environment with reduced fuel consumption and vehicle wear.

To become a goods vehicle driver you must have a high degree of skill in the handling of your vehicle, and must also be prepared to make allowances for the behaviour of others. The right attitude and approach to your driving, together with a sound knowledge of professional driving techniques and the ability to apply those techniques, are essential.

This book explains how professional drivers can obtain and maintain their Driver CPC and how the system of testing works. It also describes the ways in which some of the testing is carried out and the information that you'll require to prepare fully for all parts of the test.

The National Standard for Driving Lorries (category C) sets out the knowledge, skills and understanding that the Driver and Vehicle Standards Agency (DVSA) believes are required to be a safe and responsible driver of a category C vehicle. To read or download the national standards for driving, please visit **www.gov.uk**

The Driver CPC qualification should improve the image of all those involved in driving and operating goods vehicles, enhance the reputation of driving professionals and increase the confidence that the public and other road users have in them.

DVSA is responsible for the implementation of Driver CPC in Great Britain on behalf of the Department for Transport, and the Driver and Vehicle Agency (DVA) led the implementation in Northern Ireland on behalf of the Department of the Environment. As well as drafting the legislation, this involved introducing the initial qualification and establishing best practice for periodic training.

How to get your Driver CPC

How you get your Driver CPC will depend on whether you're already a professional driver or are looking to become a newly qualified driver. To become a new driver, you'll need to pass the Licence Acquisition Theory Test, the Driver CPC Case Study Test, the Licence Acquisition Practical Driving Test and the Driver CPC Practical Demonstration Test. You'll then need to maintain your knowledge throughout your professional driving career by completing 35 hours of periodic training in each five-year period after that (see page 20). The syllabus for periodic training courses covers a range of subjects under the following headings: safe and fuel-efficient driving, legal requirements, health, safety, service and logistics.

Acquired rights

Existing drivers, of course, will already have gained valuable experience in their work as professional drivers and these skills are reflected in the testing process. These drivers have 'acquired' rights. This means that a driver who already held a vocational driving licence on the relevant start dates was automatically deemed to hold Driver CPC. They don't need to take any new tests, but will need to do 35 hours of periodic training every five years to continue being a professional driver of a goods vehicle.

If they wish, drivers with acquired rights can now choose to take the initial Driver CPC qualification instead of periodic training to gain their first Driver Qualification Card (DQC, sometimes called a Driver CPC card).

To renew their DQC, however, they will still need to complete 35 hours of periodic training every 5 years.

Licence requirements

There are some requirements that you must satisfy before you can consider training to be a lorry driver. The minimum age for driving vehicles in category C (and its sub-categories) is reduced to 18 where the person driving

- has a Driver CPC qualification authorising the driving of a vehicle in that class
- is authorised by a document showing participation in a National Vocational Training (NVT) course to drive a vehicle in that class
- is taking lessons as a provisional licence holder and/or taking a licence acquisition test to drive a vehicle in that class.

You must also

- meet the eyesight and medical requirements
- hold a full category B driving licence
- hold a provisional LGV driving licence entitlement in the category that you wish to drive.

Drivers can take the Licence Acquisition Practical Driving Test and the Driver CPC Practical Demonstration Test in either order. If you're under 21 years old, you must pass both the licence acquisition and Driver CPC tests before you're legally allowed to drive these vehicles on the road. The only exception to this is if you're registered on an NVT course.

Who needs to obtain Driver CPC?

Not everyone who drives a goods vehicle will need to obtain the Driver CPC qualification. Only those who wish to drive large or medium-sized goods vehicles for a living will need it.

Drivers who don't need the qualification for goods vehicles are listed in section 2.

Conversion test

Drivers who hold Driver CPC for either LGV (carriage of goods) or PCV (carriage of fare-paying passengers) and who wish to broaden or modify their activities by acquiring the other vocational category of licence may choose to sit a Module 2 conversion test. This won't include the common parts of the initial Driver CPC qualification that they've already taken.

drivercpc®
GETQUALIFIEDSTAYQUALIFIED

What's in the test?

Section 2 (Gaining and maintaining your Driver CPC) describes the testing process. You should refer to the list of publications in section 6 (Further information) for full details of the theory and practice of driving goods vehicles.

New drivers need to take all of the four modules described in the panel opposite, which are collectively known as the initial test. The initial test involves a total of four hours of theory testing and two hours of practical testing. The tests are at the equivalent of National Vocational Qualification (NVQ) level two (SVQ in Scotland).

The tests are in separate modules, so that drivers can obtain their vocational category C and Driver CPC at the same time. The Driver CPC syllabus covers the additional knowledge that a professional driver needs to have. It isn't just about practical driving skills.

The theoretical side of the Driver CPC test is in two modules: the Licence Acquisition Theory Test and the Driver CPC Case Study Test. These tests are conducted on screen at approved testing centres, and can be taken together or separately. The multiple choice test consists of 100 questions.

> **The licence acquisition process**
>
> In order to drive a goods vehicle professionally, drivers need to complete the following four modules:
>
> - Licence Acquisition Theory Test, which consists of a multiple choice part and a hazard perception part (Module 1)
> - Driver CPC Case Study Test (Module 2)
> - Licence Acquisition Practical Driving Test (Module 3)
> - Driver CPC Practical Demonstration Test (Module 4).

The licence acquisition tests

These are summarised in section 3. To prepare for the Licence Acquisition Theory Test, we strongly recommend that you study the following publications.

- *The Official DVSA Theory Test for Drivers of Large Vehicles* (book, eBook, DVD-ROM, download) The only official theory test revision guide for goods vehicle, bus and coach drivers. This title combines essential background information with hundreds of official revision questions on the topics included in the test.

- *The Official Highway Code* (book, eBook, iPhone app) This is essential reading for all road users. Even if you studied it when you took your car test, it's important that you obtain an up-to-date copy to ensure that you have the most recent advice on road safety and the laws that apply to all road users.

- *Know Your Traffic Signs* This contains the vast majority of signs and road markings that you're likely to encounter.

- *The Official DVSA Guide to Driving Goods Vehicles* This book covers all aspects of driving goods vehicles, in particular the regulations and the way in which they differ from driving smaller vehicles. It also contains the practical test syllabus.

- *The Official DVSA Guide to Driving – the essential skills* This contains much general advice about driving that isn't necessarily repeated in *The Official DVSA Guide to Driving Goods Vehicles*.

To prepare for the Licence Acquisition Hazard Perception Test, we strongly recommend that you study *The Official DVSA Guide to Hazard Perception (DVD-ROM)*, which is packed with useful tips, quizzes and expert advice. It also includes more than 100 interactive hazard perception clips and your performance will receive a score so you'll know if you're ready to pass.

Before taking the Licence Acquisition Practical Driving Test, you should study *The Official DVSA Guide to Driving Goods Vehicles* for the full syllabus.

The Driver CPC Case Study Test

This tests your knowledge by presenting a series of practical scenarios that you may meet in your work and then asking questions to test your understanding. The case study testing method is described in section 4, along with the areas of the syllabus that apply to this part of the test. The books listed above will help you with the Driver CPC Case Study Test.

The Driver CPC Practical Demonstration Test

This tests your knowledge of your vehicle and how it should be operated safely and efficiently. The test will be conducted using the vehicle you present on the day. You'll be asked questions in order to demonstrate to the examiner

- what must be done before the vehicle leaves the depot to make sure that the journey is safe

- that your driving complies with all the relevant regulations

- that your driving is carried out in an eco-efficient and environmentally friendly way.

The Driver CPC Practical Demonstration Test is dealt with in detail in section 5.

section **two**

GAINING AND MAINTAINING YOUR DRIVER CPC

This section covers
- Becoming a professional driver
- Exemptions
- The tests
- Periodic training
- Documentation
- Enforcement

Becoming a professional driver

The tests that you need to take depend on the reason why your qualification to drive goods vehicles is being obtained.

If you want to be a professional driver (which means you'll drive for a living), you need to take the full test. This is divided into four modules. These parts test your knowledge of theory and your practical driving ability, but also apply your knowledge to practical situations, to make sure that you have an understanding of how to deal with the range of scenarios that you might meet in your work as a professional goods vehicle driver.

Driver CPC aims not only to improve your knowledge and skills when you start work, but also to ensure that your skills are developed throughout your working life as a professional driver. Driver CPC is expected to improve road safety and reduce casualties by ensuring that professional drivers of goods vehicles are better qualified.

Once qualified, you'll be issued with a Driver Qualification Card (DQC), which shows that you hold Driver CPC. You must carry this card at all times when driving professionally.

Exemptions

Certain drivers who need to hold goods vehicle driving licences are exempt from the requirements of the Directive and don't need to hold Driver CPC. The exemptions apply only if you're carrying out certain duties. For example, if you're employed by the armed forces you won't be required to hold Driver CPC when engaged in duties relating to that profession. However, if you leave the armed forces and are employed by a haulage company as a professional driver, you'll need to hold Driver CPC. The exemptions currently apply to drivers of

- vehicles with a maximum authorised speed not exceeding 27 mph (45 km/h)
- vehicles used by, or under the control of, the armed forces, civil defence, fire services, the prison service and forces responsible for maintaining public order
- vehicles undergoing road tests for technical development, repair or maintenance purposes, or new or rebuilt vehicles that haven't yet been put into service
- vehicles used in states of emergency or assigned to rescue missions
- vehicles used in the course of driving lessons for any person wishing to obtain a driving licence or Driver CPC, as provided for in Article 6 and Article 8(1) of Directive 2003/59/EC
- vehicles used for non-commercial carriage of passengers or goods, for personal use

- vehicles carrying material or equipment to be used by the driver in the course of his or her work, provided that driving the vehicle isn't the driver's principal activity.

You also won't need to have Driver CPC if you're not a professional driver but your work includes an incidental element of driving empty lorries, buses and coaches in the local area. You'll need to satisfy all of the following conditions:

- the vehicle is being driven by a person whose principal activity in the course of their work is not driving relevant vehicles
- you're driving within 100 km of your base
- you're not carrying any passengers
- insofar as the vehicle may be carrying goods or burden, the goods or burden must only be equipment, including machinery, that is permanently fixed to the vehicle.

If you, the driver, consider that you should be exempted from Driver CPC, then it's your responsibility to check that this is the case. You're strongly recommended to seek legal advice if you're in any doubt. Any perceived exemptions can ultimately be tested in a court of law.

The tests

Licence Acquisition Theory Test

The multiple choice part of the theory test has 100 questions and the hazard perception part has 19 clips (with 20 scorable hazards). In total, the two parts will last for 2 hours and 30 minutes.

You can take both parts one after the other on the same day, or on separate occasions, but you must pass both before taking the practical driving test. If you're a new goods vehicle driver, you must take these two parts, whether or not you intend to drive professionally.

Driver CPC Case Study Test

In addition to passing the theory test, if you wish to obtain your Driver CPC and drive professionally, you need to pass the Driver CPC Case Study Test. Each case study is based on a real-life scenario that you may encounter while driving professionally. The case study method tests your knowledge and understanding by examining how you put your skills into practice.

Questions are based around these scenarios. You'll be asked either to select from multiple choice answers or to respond by clicking on an area of a photograph or image.

There will be between six and eight case studies, each with between five and ten questions. The test, including the introductory screens, will last for 1 hour and 30 minutes.

The Official DVSA Guide to Driving Goods Vehicles and the other publications listed on pages 12–13 provide information to help you answer questions in the Driver CPC Case Study Test. It's likely to be information that you've already learned while preparing for the other parts of the test.

The case studies are a way of testing that you're able to put your knowledge and skills into practice and make judgements based on what you've learned. You must pass the Driver CPC Case Study Test before taking the Driver CPC Practical Demonstration Test.

Licence Acquisition Practical Driving Test

You'll need to pass this test if you're a new goods vehicle driver. The test lasts about 90 minutes, allowing you to show the examiner how you drive in a wide range of situations and on different types of road.

Ecosafe driving is a recognised and proven style of driving that improves road safety while reducing fuel consumption and emissions. You'll be assessed on your ecosafe driving during the test.

Driver CPC Practical Demonstration Test

This is also a practical test, but it's only for new professional drivers who need to obtain their Driver CPC. It assesses your knowledge and abilities on matters of safety and security. For example, you'll be required to show the examiner that you have knowledge of the following

- safe use of your vehicle, and the checks that you should perform on the vehicle before driving
- safe and secure loading
- how to check that your vehicle is secure from criminal acts, including human trafficking
- how to assess emergencies and risks.

Periodic training

The emphasis of Driver CPC is on maintaining your standards and enhancing your skills as your professional experience grows. In addition to ongoing training in specific driving skills, professional drivers undertaking the periodic training courses are likely to receive instruction in other matters that relate to driving goods vehicles, such as efficient and eco-friendly driving and the place of the goods vehicle in the transport system as a whole.

There are no tests for periodic training. You're required to attend approved courses for 35 hours in each five-year period. These courses must be in periods of seven hours at a time. It's considered best practice to spread your periodic training by taking one course per year, as part of a programme of continuous professional development.

The training provided must involve interaction or contact time with the trainer, and the trainer should demonstrate appropriate knowledge of the subject and deliver this in line with the approved course layout. They should understand the specific needs of individuals and encourage group participation by using various styles of questions that are relevant to the course. The trainer should check the group understands the training and provide opportunities for questions or clarification. So, although e-learning could be useful as a training tool, it must be overseen by a trainer. This means that distance learning alone isn't acceptable as training, because it can't be overseen in the correct way.

There's no set method of delivering or undertaking periodic training. It may be given in the classroom or in vehicles, or a mixture of both. It can be whatever suits your needs at the time – but it has to be approved training, by a centre approved by the Driver and Vehicle Standards Agency (DVSA), and overseen by an instructor.

'Periodic training' means regular and ongoing sessions of instruction that all vocational drivers are required to undertake in five-year cycles throughout their driving career. This should ensure that every professional driver has the opportunity to regularly gain new skills and refresh existing ones.

It's recommended that all professional drivers who regularly work in an urban environment undertake periodic training focused on safe urban driving or vulnerable road users. Safely navigating modern urban environments can be challenging for drivers of large vehicles; regular training can help to reduce the risks.

For professional drivers qualified to drive goods vehicles as well as buses and coaches, only one set of periodic training (totalling 35 hours) needs to be taken in each five-year period. So, if you qualify to drive both kinds of vehicle, you only need to take one lot of periodic training to maintain your professional qualification. You need to select the course best suited to your needs. This can be a mixture of LGV- and PCV-related subjects.

Periodic training may count as work under the Working Time Directive (WTD). If you're paid by your employer while you attend the training, the training will count as working time.

The quality of periodic training is managed through the Joint Approvals Unit for Periodic Training (JAUPT), on behalf of DVSA and the Driver and Vehicle Agency (DVA). DVSA and JAUPT will work together to monitor compliance and ensure good practice through quality assurance and the approval process. Additionally, employers are seeing road-safety and financial benefits from periodic training and can tailor the training to meet their business needs by choosing suitable providers.

It's the responsibility of training providers to deliver courses that comply with the regulations and meet employers' needs. However, employers are encouraged to discuss their expectations with providers so that courses are tailored, where possible, to meet their requirements. For example, businesses with high fuel costs might consider ecosafe driving courses, while those wishing to reduce road incidents might consider courses on safe urban driving.

UK licence holders should be aware that all periodic training is recorded on a central database system provided by DVSA. When your approved training body has uploaded your 35 hours of periodic training, your DQC will be sent to you automatically by DVLA. Any periodic training in excess of 35 hours within any five-year period **won't** count towards your next DQC and this information will be visible to trainers using the system.

Once you've obtained your Driver CPC qualification, you should ensure that your periodic training has been recorded by registering online at **www.gov.uk**

If you've attended training that hasn't been uploaded to your online record within five working days of the date of course completion, you should contact your approved training body.

Documentation

Any professional driver holding Driver CPC and keeping it up to date must prove, at certain times, that they have the Driver CPC qualification – for example, when applying for a new driving job, or if it's necessary for any other reason to show that they're qualified while driving. This proof will take the form of the Driver Qualification Card (DQC) – a plastic card that you must carry at all times when driving professionally.

New drivers

If you're a newly qualified driver with a GB (or NI) photocard licence, you'll get your DQC automatically when you've passed all four modules in the testing system – a similar process to the automated issuing of driving licences.

Existing drivers

Drivers who hold a full GB (or NI) photocard licence automatically receive their DQC when they've completed their 35 hours of training. Your DQC is sent to the address on your driving licence, so it's important to keep the address up to date. You can do this at **www.gov.uk/change-address-driving-licence**

If you're a driver who doesn't hold a full GB (or NI) photocard licence (or a driver who holds a licence from another EU member state), you may have to submit an application form to DVSA, and you may have to pay a fee for your DQC.

If your DQC is lost, stolen or damaged, you must report it to DVSA as soon as possible and apply for a replacement card.

To apply for a replacement card, call DVSA on 0300 123 7721. This line is open Monday to Friday, 8am to 5pm.

You'll be asked for your

- driving licence number
- address.

You'll also need to pay the fee via credit/debit card. The payment cardholder must be present when you call.

A DQC can only be issued to the driving licence address that DVLA currently has registered for you. It's therefore important that you keep your licence address up to date.

For more information, **visit www.gov.uk**

Once you've applied for a replacement DQC, you'll be able to continue to drive professionally while you wait for your new DQC to arrive. If your replacement card doesn't arrive within 20 days of you making the application, we strongly recommend that you contact us to confirm that your application has been received and is being processed.

If you still have a paper licence, you'll have to update it to a photocard licence before DVSA can issue your DQC. By doing so, you'll automatically receive your DQC at no cost once you've passed the Driver CPC initial qualification or completed 35 hours of periodic training.

Drivers can apply to exchange their licence online or by post. For more information on how to exchange your paper licence, visit **www.gov.uk**

Enforcement

It's an offence for an operator to cause or permit a driver who needs a DQC to drive without one, and there are penalties for drivers and operators who do this.

Driver CPC is enforced on the road in the same way as the requirement to hold an appropriate driving licence, particularly by the police, DVSA, DVLA, and the Driver and Vehicle Agency (DVA) in Northern Ireland.

Any EU enforcement body can ask a driver for proof that their Driver CPC status is current while driving in other member states, and can issue a penalty if the driver is in breach of the Directive's obligations.

EU nationals from other member states driving goods vehicles in the UK aren't affected by UK Driver CPC and don't need to carry the UK DQC. Instead, they must carry whatever their home country uses as evidence of Driver CPC competence.

Foreign nationals from non-EU countries will need to achieve UK Driver CPC if resident in the UK.

section **three**
LICENCE ACQUISITION TESTS

This section covers
- Preparing for the tests
- The theory test
- The practical driving test

Preparing for the tests

All new drivers wishing to drive goods vehicles must pass the appropriate theory test (two parts) before taking the practical driving test. Although you can start your lessons before passing the theory test, you can't book the practical driving test until you've passed the theory test (also called Module 1).

The two parts of the theory test – the multiple choice part and the hazard perception part – can be taken either on the same day or on separate occasions.

The Licence Acquisition Practical Driving Test (Module 3) includes an eco-driving assessment.

Full details of these tests and the skills and knowledge they cover are given in *The Official DVSA Theory Test for Drivers of Large Vehicles* (book, eBook, DVD-ROM or download), *The Official DVSA Guide to Driving Goods Vehicles*, *Know Your Traffic Signs* and *The Official Highway Code* (book, eBook or iPhone app). These publications will help you study for the relevant tests.

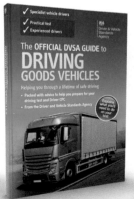

The theory test

Your training for the theory test should cover a comprehensive knowledge of *The Official Highway Code*, *The Official DVSA Guide to Driving – the essential skills, Know Your Traffic Signs,* and *The Official DVSA Guide to Driving Goods Vehicles*. Such training includes

- the regulations governing drivers' permitted working hours (EC Directive 561/2006)
- regulations governing the carriage of goods by road
- general motoring regulations
- health and safety regulations.

For more information, go to **www.gov.uk**

You should refer to *The Official DVSA Theory Test for Drivers of Large Vehicles* (book, eBook, DVD-ROM or download) for full details of what this section of the qualification involves. This test (both the multiple choice and hazard perception parts) is taken by candidates who want to obtain either a vocational licence only, or a vocational licence and Driver CPC. In the latter case, candidates also take the Driver CPC Case Study Test.

The theory test consists of 100 multiple choice questions and 19 hazard perception clips (with 20 scorable hazards). The multiple choice part lasts for two hours and the hazard perception part lasts for 30 minutes.

The purpose of the theory test is to assess your knowledge and skills over the complete range of matters that affect drivers of goods vehicles. The test is taken on screen at an approved testing centre.

The theory test pass results, for either the multiple choice or hazard perception part of the test, have a life of two years. You need to hold a valid pass result for both parts of the theory test to be able to book and take your practical driving test. This means that if you don't pass the practical driving test within two years of passing the theory test, you'll have to retake and pass the theory test before you can book the practical driving test.

There are some specific rules for certain types of vehicle, and for vehicles with certain kinds of trailer. *The Official DVSA Guide to Driving Goods Vehicles* contains full details of what you can drive once you've passed the theory and practical tests. That guide also contains details of the various kinds of licence that are available for all drivers of goods vehicles and the classes of vehicle in each category.

The practical driving test

All goods vehicle drivers must take this test, even if they don't intend to drive professionally and don't need to take the full set of tests for Driver CPC.

The Licence Acquisition Practical Driving Test (Module 3) is an assessment of your ability to drive safely.

This module will test your practical driving skills in the following areas

- vehicle controls, equipment and components
- behaviour on the road
- vehicle characteristics
- road and weather conditions
- traffic signs, rules and regulations
- vehicle control and procedures
- safe working practices
- motorway driving.

The Official DVSA Guide to Driving Goods Vehicles contains lots of information and advice to help you prepare for the practical test.

The driving part of the test will last a minimum of 60 minutes on the road.

In your practical driving training, you must appreciate the differences between driving large vehicles and small vehicles. Some of these differences will be obvious from the moment you start to drive a larger vehicle. Others will only become apparent as you gain more experience during your training.

Ecosafe driving

As a professional driver, you have a responsibility to use your vehicle in a manner that's sympathetic to the environment. *The Official DVSA Guide to Driving Goods Vehicles* contains full information on ecosafe driving. If you follow the principles of driving with eco-awareness, you'll become a more environmentally friendly driver. Your journeys will be more comfortable for you, and you could considerably reduce the amount of fuel your vehicle uses, thereby reducing those emissions that damage the atmosphere, as well as saving on fuel costs. You'll also be setting a professional example to other road users.

One of the main ways to be an ecosafe driver is to plan ahead, so that you're prepared for potential hazards. Your ecosafe driving instruction will show you the ways in which this is done in practice, while keeping in mind your safety and that of other road users as you're driving.

Remember that during the practical driving test you'll be assessed on your ecosafe driving. The examiner may give you some advice to help you improve your ecosafe driving skills.

You can improve fuel economy while driving
by remembering the following factors.

E very time you move off, do so smoothly – avoid harsh acceleration.

C hange down to the appropriate gear, but wait while speed decreases.

O n acceleration, try to skip gears where you can.

N ever leave it to chance – maintain your vehicle in good condition.

O bserve and keep within the rev counter green zone.

M inimise brake use – plan ahead and keep monitoring road conditions.

Y our speed should remain constant when possible.

section **four**
THE CASE STUDY TEST

This section covers
- The case study test
- What to expect on the day
- What you need to know
- Case study example

The case study test

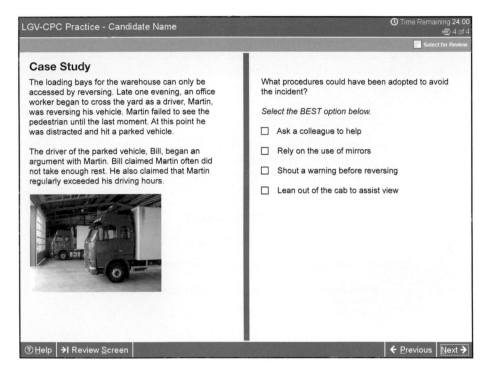

⏱ Time Remaining 24:00
≋ 4 of 4
▢ Select for Review

Case Study

The loading bays for the warehouse can only be accessed by reversing. Late one evening, an office worker began to cross the yard as a driver, Martin, was reversing his vehicle. Martin failed to see the pedestrian until the last moment. At this point he was distracted and hit a parked vehicle.

The driver of the parked vehicle, Bill, began an argument with Martin. Bill claimed Martin often did not take enough rest. He also claimed that Martin regularly exceeded his driving hours.

What procedures could have been adopted to avoid the incident?

Select the BEST option below.

☐ Ask a colleague to help

☐ Rely on the use of mirrors

☐ Shout a warning before reversing

☐ Lean out of the cab to assist view

⑦ Help | →I Review Screen | ← Previous | Next →

The case studies are designed to assess

- knowledge (recall of facts)
- comprehension (understanding)
- application (practical use of knowledge and understanding).

This is done by presenting a scenario or a set of circumstances that you may encounter in your working life as a professional goods vehicle driver. You'll then be asked a number of questions relating to this scenario, which will require you to consider how you would react/behave in each case.

The look and feel of the actual case study screens may have changed since this book went to press.

The Official DVSA Guide to Driving Goods Vehicles and other publications listed on pages 12–13 provide information to help you answer questions in the case studies.

What to expect on the day

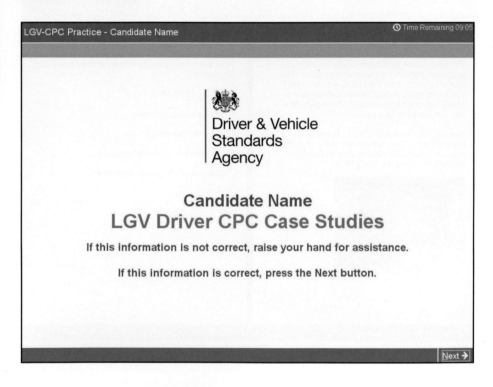

Driver & Vehicle Standards Agency

Candidate Name

LGV Driver CPC Case Studies

If this information is not correct, raise your hand for assistance.

If this information is correct, press the Next button.

Next →

The case studies part of the initial Driver CPC qualification will last for 90 minutes. You'll be given 15 minutes to acquaint yourself with the system and 75 minutes to answer questions. During that time you're required to review between six and eight different case studies, each with between five and ten questions attached to them. You'll need to answer 50 questions in total.

You'll use a visual display unit (VDU) similar to the one used for the multiple choice and hazard perception tests. You'll need to touch the screen or use the mouse to guide the cursor and touch or click on certain areas of the screen to record your answers.

The following introductory screens are shown at the beginning of the test so that you can familiarise yourself with the test procedure.

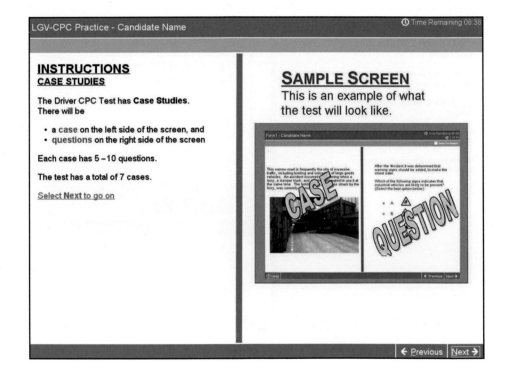

INSTRUCTIONS
BUTTONS

To go to the next question or screen, select the Next button.

If you wish to go back, select the Previous button.

If you don't know what to do, select the Help button.

When you are finished, select the **End Test** button.

Select **Next** to go on

SAMPLE SCREEN
This is what the test buttons will look like.

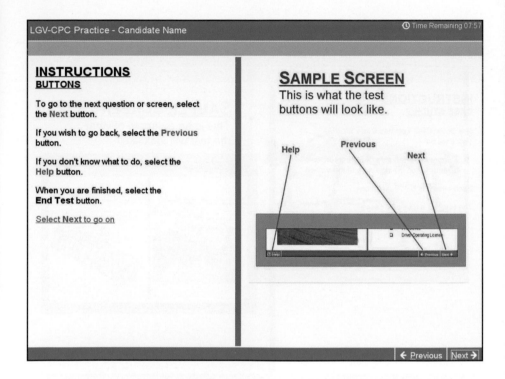

← Previous　|　Next →

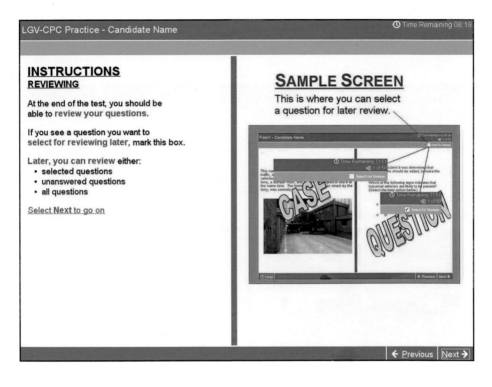

You'll be presented with a set of facts – the case study – which will appear on the left-hand side of the screen. The set of facts or scenario will be presented in a text format with a supporting picture or diagram. As you move within the case study and answer each question, you can be assured that the facts and the scenario content won't change, although you do have the opportunity to re-read the scenario throughout the case study should you wish to do so.

The questions will appear, one by one, on the right-hand side of the screen, and you'll be asked to respond in various ways. There are four methods of answering the questions; the following slides show examples.

1. Multiple choice Choosing one correct answer from a number of options.

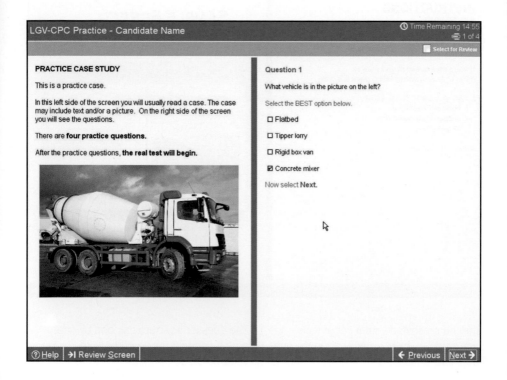

☐ Select for Review

PRACTICE CASE STUDY

This is a practice case.

In this left side of the screen you will usually read a case. The case may include text and/or a picture. On the right side of the screen you will see the questions.

There are **four practice questions.**

After the practice questions, **the real test will begin.**

Question 1

What vehicle is in the picture on the left?

Select the BEST option below.

☐ Flatbed

☐ Tipper lorry

☐ Rigid box van

☑ Concrete mixer

Now select **Next.**

⑦ Help ↦I Review Screen

← Previous   Next →

2. **Multi-response** Selecting more than
   one correct answer from a number of
   options.

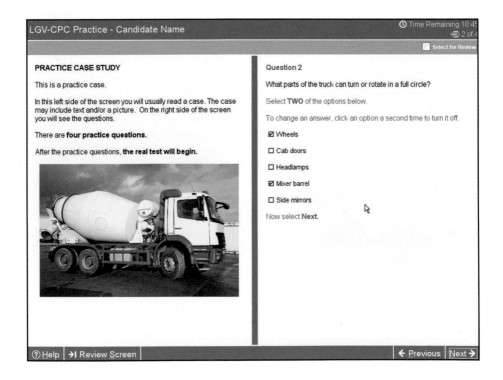

3. Audio Listening to an audio clip, then choosing one correct answer from a number of options.

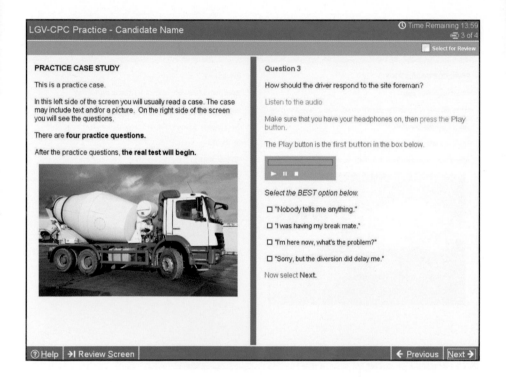

☐ Select for Review

PRACTICE CASE STUDY

This is a practice case.

In this left side of the screen you will usually read a case. The case may include text and/or a picture. On the right side of the screen you will see the questions.

There are **four practice questions.**

After the practice questions, **the real test will begin.**

Question 3

How should the driver respond to the site foreman?

Listen to the audio

Make sure that you have your headphones on, then press the Play button.

The Play button is the first button in the box below.

▶ ‖ ■

Select the BEST option below.

☐ "Nobody tells me anything."

☐ "I was having my break mate."

☐ "I'm here now, what's the problem?"

☐ "Sorry, but the diversion did delay me."

Now select **Next**.

⑦ Help ⤒ Review Screen   ← Previous   Next →

4. Hot spot Using the mouse, clicking on an appropriate area of an illustration.

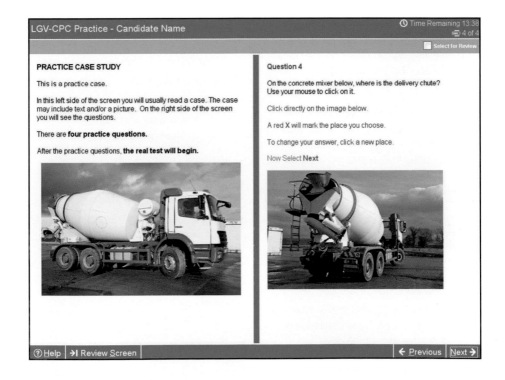

Practice You'll be given the opportunity to practise these techniques before you start the test.

Results You'll be told the result of the test within 10 minutes of its completion.

What you need to know

Driving techniques

This part of the syllabus is designed to test your understanding of how different conditions will affect your use of the accelerator, brakes and gearbox. You need to recognise good driving practice and to know that this has an effect on the stability, efficiency and fuel economy of the vehicle you're driving.

You'll also need to understand how the load you're transporting will 'move' within the vehicle when you brake, accelerate and steer away from a straight line – for example, when cornering or negotiating roundabouts.

Safe and fuel-efficient driving (SAFED)

You should know

- the basic principles of SAFED
- how to use the controls to maximise fuel efficiency. Only by understanding the characteristics of the drive and transmission system can you make efficient use of it. For example, you should understand how to use
  - the green band on the rev counter (where appropriate)
  - block gear changing (skipping or missing out gears on either up or down changes)
  - the most appropriate gears generally

- how to read and make best use of the on-board fuel consumption monitors
- the effect on vehicle safety of
  - cruise- and speed-control equipment
  - smooth use of the accelerator
  - appropriate use of the brakes (including retarders/exhaust brakes)
- how to use the safety controls in order to
  - control the vehicle
  - minimise wear and tear
  - avoid mechanical failures.

To receive SAFED training you must

- hold a valid driving licence including category C or C+E entitlements
- ideally undertake the training in a vehicle fitted with fuel-monitoring equipment.

As a training module, SAFED meets the relevant syllabus area of Driver CPC, but only when delivered by a training centre approved by JAUPT. For drivers, this means that if you intend to count your training as part of the CPC requirements, you must select a training company with JAUPT approval of both the training organisation and its SAFED course. Such approval will have a unique number issued by JAUPT.

Load safety

You should be able to

- determine styles of driving that ensure the load you carry remains stable, and that you retain control of your vehicle at all times
- recognise the effect that excessive acceleration, braking and speed can have on the way in which different types of loads may move. You should understand the effects of
  - excessive acceleration
  - harsh braking
  - fast cornering
  - too sharp a turning circle
  - changing lanes too quickly
  - veering suddenly when driving.

Other techniques

You should be able to

- recognise the benefits of good positioning on the road and know how to allow space so that you don't compromise the safety of your vehicle or load
- show that you're aware of the dimensions of your vehicle, especially where there are particular risks with side, forward and rear overhangs
- recognise the importance of making the journey as safe and smooth as possible
- recognise the factors that contribute to stress-free driving and factors that contribute to stress
- understand the distractions you may face when driving, both inside and outside the vehicle, and know how to deal with them. These distractions can include using the radio, mobile phones or other hand-held equipment, satellite-navigation devices, other drivers, weather conditions, etc. Remember that it's illegal to use a mobile phone or other hand-held device while driving.

Securing of loads

In this section you'll need to show that you recognise the different ways in which loads should be secured and the various methods that should be utilised. When securing a load you need to take into account

- the nature of the load
- the suitability of the vehicle
- the stability and positioning of the load
- the type of restraint that should be used
- protection from the weather.

You'll need to show that you can ensure your load and vehicle remain secure and stable when

- braking
- steering
- cornering

even in emergency situations.

You must demonstrate that you know how to check that

- all devices for securing the load are effective
- ropes, chains and straps are secure and free from visible fault or damage
- sheets are fastened down correctly
- container-locking handles are secure
- doors, drop sides and tailgates are fastened
- hatches on tanker vehicles are closed to prevent spillage.

Load types may vary, but any load should be secured solidly, carefully and in an appropriate manner, using the most suitable anchorage points or restraining devices. These will ensure that the load doesn't move or fall from the vehicle during the journey. Types of load to be considered could include

- metal
- timber
- palletised
- loose bulk
- high
- wide
- multi-drop (varied goods).

Be aware also of your own personal security when outside your vehicle. Notice what's going on around you – for example, are there people watching nearby who seem interested in your vehicle (possible hijacking situation)? You should be especially alert if the load you're carrying has commercial value (alcohol, tobacco, electrical goods, etc).

This slide and the following slides show the way that some questions are asked in the case study.

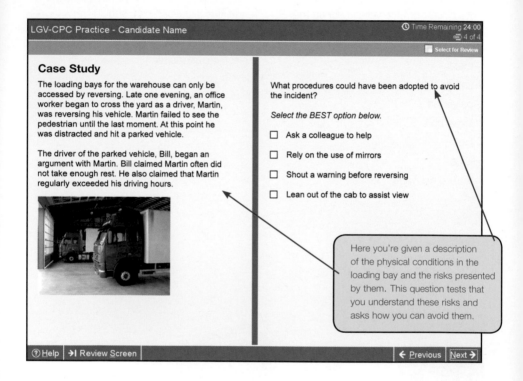

Case Study

The loading bays for the warehouse can only be accessed by reversing. Late one evening, an office worker began to cross the yard as a driver, Martin, was reversing his vehicle. Martin failed to see the pedestrian until the last moment. At this point he was distracted and hit a parked vehicle.

The driver of the parked vehicle, Bill, began an argument with Martin. Bill claimed Martin often did not take enough rest. He also claimed that Martin regularly exceeded his driving hours.

What procedures could have been adopted to avoid the incident?

Select the BEST option below.

☐ Ask a colleague to help

☐ Rely on the use of mirrors

☐ Shout a warning before reversing

☐ Lean out of the cab to assist view

Here you're given a description of the physical conditions in the loading bay and the risks presented by them. This question tests that you understand these risks and asks how you can avoid them.

⑦ Help ➔| Review Screen | ⬅ Previous | Next ➔

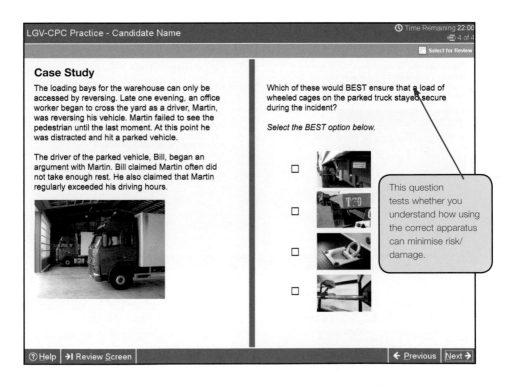

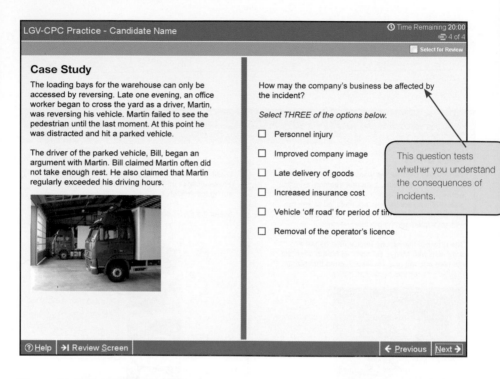

Case Study

The loading bays for the warehouse can only be accessed by reversing. Late one evening, an office worker began to cross the yard as a driver, Martin, was reversing his vehicle. Martin failed to see the pedestrian until the last moment. At this point he was distracted and hit a parked vehicle.

The driver of the parked vehicle, Bill, began an argument with Martin. Bill claimed Martin often did not take enough rest. He also claimed that Martin regularly exceeded his driving hours.

How may the company's business be affected by the incident?

Select THREE of the options below.

☐ Personnel injury

☐ Improved company image

☐ Late delivery of goods

☐ Increased insurance cost

☐ Vehicle 'off road' for period of time

☐ Removal of the operator's licence

This question tests whether you understand the consequences of incidents.

⑦ Help →| Review Screen   ← Previous Next →

Regulations that govern the carriage of various load types

This section tests your understanding not only of what the law says but also of how the law should be implemented. You should know the procedures to adopt in order to comply with the law relating to all the items and requirements listed below.

Types of load

You should be able to

- understand and comply with the law concerning the transport of loads generally, and the specific requirements that govern all types of load

- understand and apply the regulations that govern the movement of different types of loads, such as
  - dangerous goods
  - restricted goods.

Paperwork

You should know and be able to explain the paperwork legally required to be in your possession when carrying a type of load specified previously, both in the UK and abroad.

Seat belts

You should

- understand the law concerning seat belts and the requirements laid upon the company and the driver

- know the procedure in your company for checking the condition and working order of seat belts and reporting any defects. If seat belts are fitted, they must be worn at all times by you, the driver, and by any co-driver or assistant who may be travelling with you.

Safety equipment

You should

- understand and be able to explain the law concerning safety equipment, including the carrying of fire extinguishers and first aid equipment if your vehicle has them

- understand and be able to explain the correct use of warning lights, buzzers, warning systems, etc and any emergency equipment carried

- know how to check these items before taking responsibility for the vehicle and know the procedure for reporting defects (see also the section on dealing with emergencies on pages 58–59).

Vehicle maintenance

You should

- understand the requirement for vehicles to be properly maintained on a suitable schedule

- understand your role as a driver in checking for and reporting defects to the correct maintenance staff in your organisation

- check your vehicle at the start of your shift (walk-round checks, brake lines, etc).

Alcohol

You should understand the regulations relating to alcohol and driving. Be aware that alcohol may remain in the body for 24–48 hours. The effects on your reactions will be evident the next morning and will affect your ability to drive safely. Also, you could fail a breath test.

Your body tissues need up to 48 hours to recover from alcohol intake, although your breath/blood alcohol levels may appear normal after 24 hours. If you're convicted of a drink-driving offence while driving an ordinary motor vehicle, a driving ban will result in you losing your goods vehicle entitlement and your livelihood.

Regulations that govern the carriage of illegal immigrants

Vehicle security

This is a very important issue, involving heavy fines for those found to be carrying illegal immigrants. Companies are required to have an effective system in place to protect their vehicles.

You should be aware of TIR* procedures so that, when travelling outside the European Union (eg Russia) and going through customs, you can ensure that

- TIR cords are securely fitted to your vehicle

- you know the points in your journey at which you need to check the cords for signs of tampering

- you have the appropriate paperwork available throughout your journey.

You should be able to demonstrate your awareness of the requirements of the effective system and the points at which you need to check your vehicle for any security breach. Your company should provide you with relevant documentation including instructions and advice.

You also need to be able to demonstrate your awareness of the various methods of entry that could be used to gain access to vehicles.

*TIR stands for Transports Internationaux Routiers (International Road Transport). It's an international transit system allowing goods to travel across one or more international borders with the minimum of customs involvement.

Regulations that govern drivers' hours and tachographs

You'll be asked to interpret the regulations from the specific information within the case study.

You should

* know how to interpret the requirements of both EC and domestic drivers' hours regulations so that you can calculate the precise amount of time you can drive or the hours of daily or weekly rest you must take within the scenario given

* understand under which conditions the two regulations, EC and domestic, apply

* be able to interpret the requirements of the Working Time Directive and the Road Transport (Working Time) Regulations

* be able to demonstrate how to record your hours using both analogue and digital tachographs. For an analogue type, you fill in and record information on a chart. For a digital type, you insert a personal driver smart card or, if your card is lost, stolen or develops a fault,

you should produce a printout at the start and end of each day

* be able to demonstrate that you know what to do when the tachograph isn't working – always carry spare charts so that if this happens you can record your journeys/trips manually, including departure and arrival times. In the event of digital tachograph failure, you should record information on the reverse of the printout of driver activities

* understand the penalties for infringing any of the above regulations and for tampering with monitoring equipment.

You should also

* be able to demonstrate that you understand the requirements of the Driver CPC regulations

* understand the social environment and your rights and duties as a driver regarding your initial qualification and your periodic training.

Health and safety at work, both in the workplace and on the road

In the workplace

You should

- understand and be able to explain where there are risks for employees within the workplace. For example, garage flooring can be slippery, so you must always

    - wear suitable footwear

    - use dedicated walkways and safe areas

    - look out for moving vehicles, especially those reversing out between other vehicles

- know your role in promoting and maintaining health and safety and be able to explain the procedure for ensuring that the workplace is maintained in a safe condition. Everyone is responsible for

health and safety in the workplace; if you see anything hazardous, such as an oil spillage, you should report it so that it can be cleared up.

On the road

You'll be required to show that you're aware of the hazards associated with your vehicle while travelling on the road. You should also show that you know how to alert others to such risks and hazards.

You should

- know and understand how and where road traffic incidents can occur

    - on and around the vehicle (including while loading and unloading)

    - at what point during the journey

    - at both high and low speeds.

The majority of injuries will occur when drivers have to take unplanned evasive action (for example, harsh braking)

- understand the need to avoid taking unnecessary risks and to work within your capabilities. You should be able to
  - assess what level of involvement you should take in the event of an incident
  - understand that your involvement may depend on how closely you're involved with the situation (see also the separate section on dealing with emergencies on pages 58–59)
- understand that, as a professional driver, members of the public may look to you for help and guidance. You should
  - act only within your abilities and training
  - not take unacceptable risks that put yourself or others in danger
- be able to understand road incident statistics (including the location, types and causes of incidents) relating to goods vehicles

- be able to explain the consequences of road traffic incidents and how they can affect any passenger, and the employee and employer, in both human and financial terms. You should understand the consequences for
  - the driver
  - any passenger (eg co-driver/assistant)
  - your colleagues
  - the families of those involved

  in incidents of all levels of seriousness. You should be aware of the effect of incidents on the domestic and working lives of all involved, and on the organisation for which you work.

More examples of questions asked by the case study test.

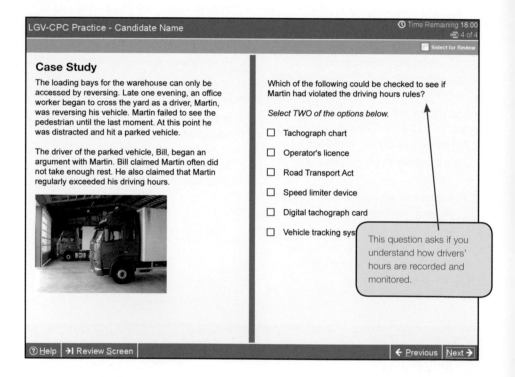

4 of 4

☐ Select for Review

Case Study

The loading bays for the warehouse can only be accessed by reversing. Late one evening, an office worker began to cross the yard as a driver, Martin, was reversing his vehicle. Martin failed to see the pedestrian until the last moment. At this point he was distracted and hit a parked vehicle.

The driver of the parked vehicle, Bill, began an argument with Martin. Bill claimed Martin often did not take enough rest. He also claimed that Martin regularly exceeded his driving hours.

Which of the following could be checked to see if Martin had violated the driving hours rules?

Select TWO of the options below.

☐ Tachograph chart

☐ Operator's licence

☐ Road Transport Act

☐ Speed limiter device

☐ Digital tachograph card

☐ Vehicle tracking sys

> This question asks if you understand how drivers' hours are recorded and monitored.

⑦ Help | ⇥I Review Screen | ← Previous | Next →

LGV-CPC Practice - Candidate Name

Time Remaining 16:00
4 of 4

Select for Review

Case Study

The loading bays for the warehouse can only be accessed by reversing. Late one evening, an office worker began to cross the yard as a driver, Martin, was reversing his vehicle. Martin failed to see the pedestrian until the last moment. At this point he was distracted and hit a parked vehicle.

The driver of the parked vehicle, Bill, began an argument with Martin. Bill claimed Martin often did not take enough rest. He also claimed that Martin regularly exceeded his driving hours.

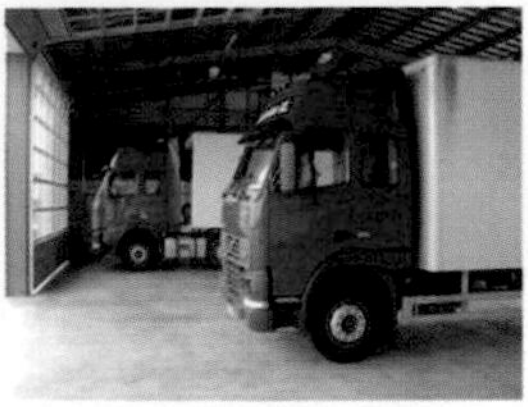

Make sure you have your headphones on then press the Play button.

The Play button is the first button in the blue box to the right.

The following is an argument between Martin and Bill.

Bill – "Look what you've done, you've hit my truck. I reckon you were asleep or drunk."

Martin – "I haven't done anything wrong, I haven't exceeded my hours and I don't drink. In fact, the only thing I've had all day is flu medicine."

Which of the following is a well-known side effect of the substance Martin took?

- ☐ Thirst
- ☐ Drowsiness
- ☐ Tunnel vision
- ☐ Ringing in the ears

Here you'll be asked to listen to the audio clip and then answer the questions that follow.

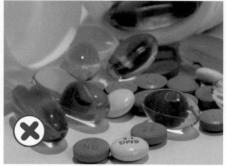

Keeping fit for the job

You should show that you know how to carry out your duties in a safe and competent manner. You also need to show that you're aware of how important it is to be healthy when driving, and what can compromise your health. You must be aware of the symptoms that might cause your standard of driving to fall to an unacceptable and unsafe level.

You should be able to

- show that you understand the effects of alcohol on your ability to drive, and the way in which alcohol can stay in the body for a long time – this may affect your ability to drive safely

- recognise the effects that some prescribed and 'over-the-counter' drugs can have on your ability to drive. Even prescribed drugs can make you drowsy and affect your driving. Always read the label and, if in doubt, seek advice or don't drive

- explain the law concerning the use of drugs and alcohol and the penalties that exist for non-compliance. Anyone caught driving while unfit/over the limit through drugs or alcohol won't only be fined heavily but will also lose their licence and may even be imprisoned

- understand the effects of any other substances likely to affect behaviour, impair judgement or increase reaction times

- show that you understand the effects on performance that different diets can produce. Being overweight causes strain on your heart and a poor diet can make you feel sluggish and tired. You should be aware of the importance of a properly balanced diet and of regular eating with respect to shift patterns

- demonstrate that you understand
  - the symptoms and causes of stress and fatigue
  - that stress and fatigue can be caused at work or at home
  - how stress and fatigue can cause personality and behavioural changes
  - what action to take to minimise the effects of stress and fatigue.

  You can become stressed by getting too agitated about situations. Being stressed can cause
  - headaches
  - high blood pressure
  - tiredness
  - irritability

  so you must try to remain calm and not allow yourself to take things out of context or to an extreme

- understand the fundamental role of the basic work/rest cycle in making you a safe and professional driver. You should understand the effect of insufficient sleep due to a variety of circumstances, including out-of-work social activity or a change in shift patterns.

YOU DRIVE FOR A LIVING BUT YOU'D KILL FOR SOME SLEEP?

Tiredness Kills. Make time for a break.
think.direct.gov.uk

THINK!

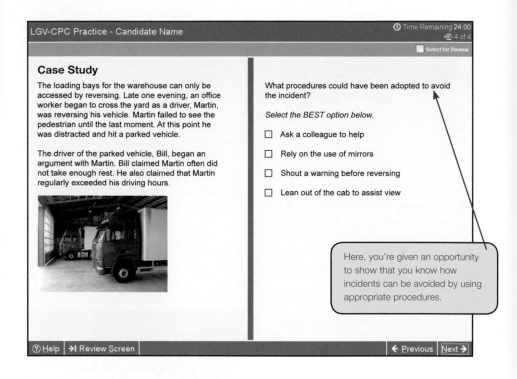

Case Study

The loading bays for the warehouse can only be accessed by reversing. Late one evening, an office worker began to cross the yard as a driver, Martin, was reversing his vehicle. Martin failed to see the pedestrian until the last moment. At this point he was distracted and hit a parked vehicle.

The driver of the parked vehicle, Bill, began an argument with Martin. Bill claimed Martin often did not take enough rest. He also claimed that Martin regularly exceeded his driving hours.

What procedures could have been adopted to avoid the incident?

Select the BEST option below.

☐ Ask a colleague to help

☐ Rely on the use of mirrors

☐ Shout a warning before reversing

☐ Lean out of the cab to assist view

> Here, you're given an opportunity to show that you know how incidents can be avoided by using appropriate procedures.

⑦ Help | →I Review Screen | ← Previous | Next →

Dealing with emergencies

You should be able to show that you would deal with an unexpected incident in an efficient and professional manner, which would ensure the safety of others involved.

You should be able to

- prioritise the actions taken if involved in an incident
- prioritise the actions taken as a witness to an incident

- demonstrate that you're aware of the procedures for investigating a possible fire and prioritising actions if you find a fire. You should know, if appropriate and following suitable training, how to use on-board firefighting equipment safely and effectively

- explain the procedures for how to prioritise casualties and give first aid, if you've received suitable training and aren't prohibited from doing so by your employer

- explain the procedures for

  - contacting the emergency services

  - contacting your operator

  - communicating specific information on casualties and the scenario

- understand the requirements of the load and the need to communicate accurate information on types of load and any hazardous materials to the emergency services. You should also know how to ask for the assistance of others at the scene or in your organisation

- demonstrate that you know how to ensure the safety of the loads you're transporting

- demonstrate that you're aware of your company's procedures to effectively record and report any incidents, including gathering or preserving relevant and supporting information and, if necessary, making sketches or taking photographs.

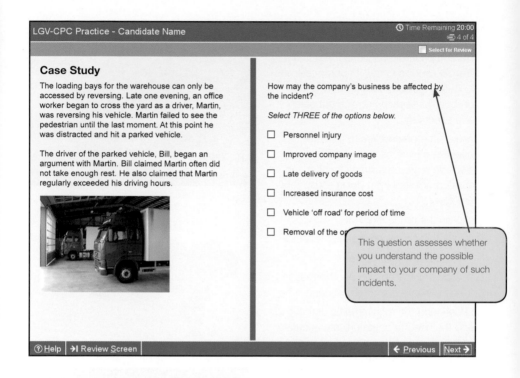

Case Study

The loading bays for the warehouse can only be accessed by reversing. Late one evening, an office worker began to cross the yard as a driver, Martin, was reversing his vehicle. Martin failed to see the pedestrian until the last moment. At this point he was distracted and hit a parked vehicle.

The driver of the parked vehicle, Bill, began an argument with Martin. Bill claimed Martin often did not take enough rest. He also claimed that Martin regularly exceeded his driving hours.

How may the company's business be affected by the incident?

Select THREE of the options below.

☐ Personnel injury

☐ Improved company image

☐ Late delivery of goods

☐ Increased insurance cost

☐ Vehicle 'off road' for period of time

☐ Removal of the op

> This question assesses whether you understand the possible impact to your company of such incidents.

The role of the driver within the company/organisation

This section requires you to recognise your role and the way it interacts with others in the organisation for which you work. You also need to understand how your performance can affect the perception that other road users have of the whole industry.

You should

- be able to recognise the importance of your role as a driver and the limits of your responsibilities. Your company's image will be enhanced by

  - your safe driving practices

  - adoption of a positive attitude to others

  - your promotion of the company and the industry generally

- understand the importance of good customer care and taking part in any driver development programmes that are available through your company or organisation, or independently

- understand that the way in which goods vehicle drivers carry out their duties to their company and its clients can create a positive or negative image of the industry. You should also understand
  - all the routes and schedules that you'll work
  - the structure of the company
  - the company procedures that affect or are affected by its drivers
- know the categories of people you'll meet, both inside and outside the organisation, and with whom you may have to work in the course of your duties. These can include
  - line managers
  - other drivers
  - the public
  - customers
  - the authorities.

  You should be able to show that you know how to relate to other occupations within the organisation
- understand the role of the driver. You should know the requirements of the job, namely
  - the loading, carriage and delivery of goods safely and securely and in a timely manner
  - the importance of your presentation as a representative of the company
  - the presentation of your vehicle.

  You should take pride in your role in your organisation and understand the value you bring to it

- be able to demonstrate that you're aware of the need for walk-round checks and the procedures that should be adopted for carrying them out and when finding faults that need to be rectified
- be able to recognise and explain the nature of the organisation and why goods are carried in different ways
- be able to recognise the main sources of income and costs
- understand the main methods used for communicating within the organisation. You should also know
  - how to deal with on-the-spot customer complaints
  - how to pass complaints on, where appropriate and in a satisfactory way, to others in your organisation with responsibility for dealing with them if you can't
- understand the commercial and financial effects of a dispute affecting your organisation. As a driver, you may be involved in industrial action or be affected by the disputes of others. You should understand the effects of this on
  - the company
  - your colleagues
  - your customers
  - the industry generally.

  You should also understand the consequences, which may include
  - the loss of customers
  - the transfer of custom to competitors or other methods of freight transport

and that this effect may be temporary or permanent. You should also be aware of the possible financial or legal implications of various kinds of industrial action.

Freight transport organisation

This section tests your understanding of the way in which road haulage and freight transport fit into the transport industry of the United Kingdom. You'll be required to demonstrate that you know how the industry compares to other types of freight transportation, who operates within the industry and how it's organised. You'll also need to demonstrate an awareness of specialisations and developments within the industry. You should

- know how road transport relates to other modes of freight transport and how this compares to rail freight, air freight, canals, intermodal and shipping

  - road transport accounts for 68% of all domestic freight transport in Great Britain while rail freight accounts for 9% and waterborne carriage 19%

  - 93% of freight by road is moved by goods vehicles and 7% by vans

- know about the different types of road transport activity; for example

  - transport for hire or reward, own-account, auxiliary activity and understand the differences between them

- goods vehicle freight activity is undertaken by either hauliers (who carry goods for profit) or own-account operators who carry their own goods

- 64% of freight moved by goods vehicles is undertaken by hauliers and 36% by own-account operators

- the role of third-party carriers has progressively widened from goods movement to the management of supply chains for their customers

- understand the differences between the types of activity carried out; for example, between hire and reward, own-account, trunking to hubs, use of fork-lift trucks, clearing houses, freight forwarders and groupage operators

- be able to understand the organisation of the main types of transport company, such as sole traders, partnerships, private and public limited companies and their auxiliary transport activities, such as multi-drop, trunking, subcontracting and route planning

  - the road transport industry in the UK is made up of relatively few large multinational companies operating many thousands of goods vehicles, plus a large number of small businesses operating fleets of less than five goods vehicles

  - some 60,000 businesses operate goods vehicles in the UK. Less than 500 operate more than 100 goods vehicles

- know about and understand the difference between transport specialisations and specialist operations such as container transport, mixer vehicles, car transporters, temperature-controlled vehicles, hazardous goods, demountable bodies, abnormal loads, skips and tippers, and livestock carriers. Specialisations include

  - specific sectors of the marketplace, often reflecting the nature of the goods and the skills and equipment needed to handle them (eg dangerous goods, livestock, temperature-controlled transport, parcels)

  - specific segments of the supply chain (eg trunking, intermodal container operations from ports, end-delivery to consumers)

  - geographical specialisations: pallet networks use a group of hauliers, each with a strong regional presence, to create a national distribution system

  - those offering global supply-chain solutions, providing end-to-end deliveries using a combination of transport modes (integrators)

- have an awareness of changes to the industry, such as diversification of services provided, shifts in rail-road usage and subcontracting. You should also be aware of industry trends, including the provision of supply-chain services such as barcoding, packaging and labelling, warehousing, and stuffing/unstuffing of containers. Be aware that

  - carriers are often embedded within their customers' supply chains, underpinned by the stability of long-term contracts

  - longer-term contracts have also enabled carriers to be more proactive in investing in specialist equipment that optimises load fill and minimises handling, providing the initiative for collaborative working where two customers' product and freight movements can be handled together

- have an awareness of changes driven by environmental factors, such as the increasing use of alternative fuels, the impact of engine emissions and appropriate gearbox usage.

63

Case study example

Here's an example of how one full case study will look during your test.

Please note that you won't be asked these example questions in your real test.

Note that five example questions are given here, but in the real test you'll have to answer between five and ten questions for each case study.

Answers to this case study example test are given on page 82.

Case Study

The case will appear on each screen.
The case will have 5–10 questions.
Read the case, it will help you answer the questions.

To begin this case study, select **Next**.

| Previous (P) | Next (N) | Review Screen (S) | | Help (H) | End Test (E) |

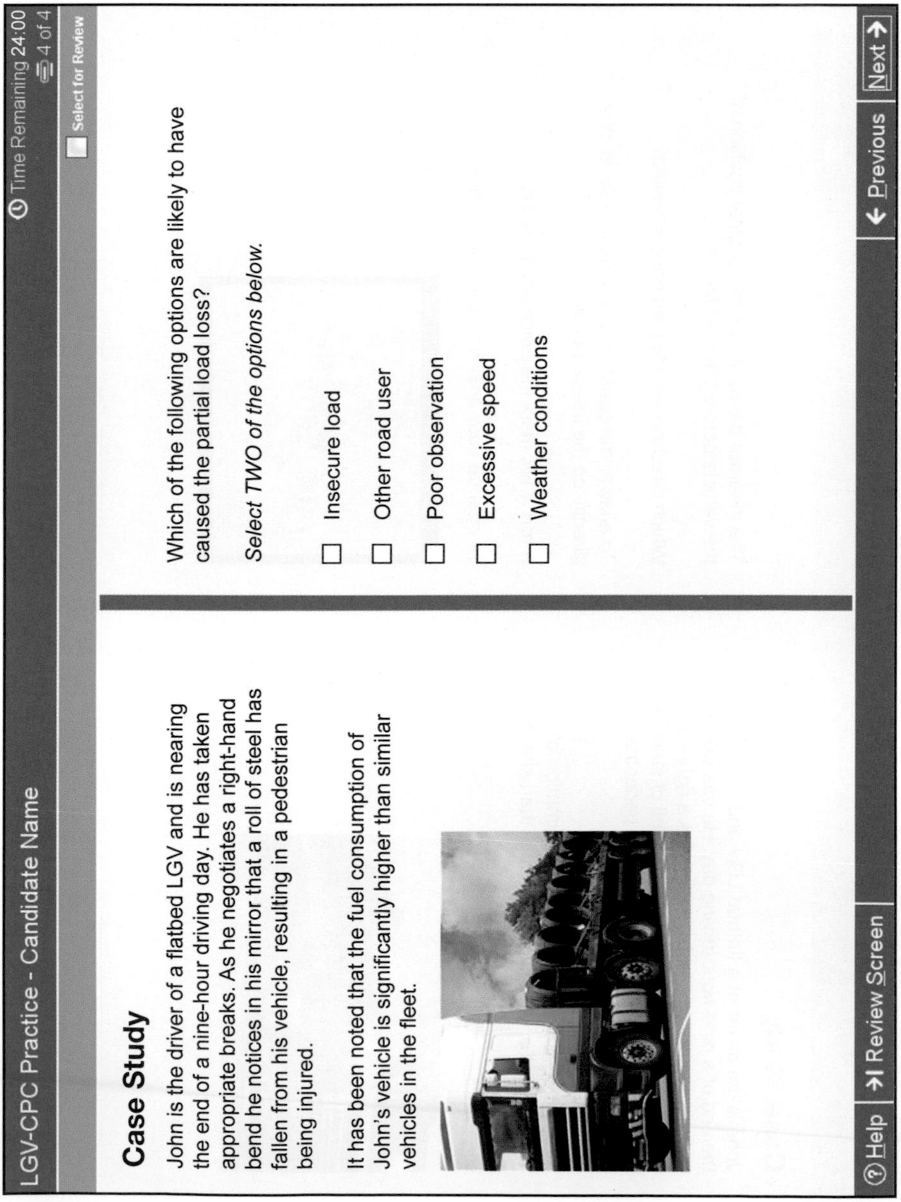

LGV-CPC Practice - Candidate Name
Time Remaining 24:00
4 of 4
Select for Review
Case Study
John is the driver of a flatbed LGV and is nearing the end of a nine-hour driving day. He has taken appropriate breaks. As he negotiates a right-hand bend he notices in his mirror that a roll of steel has fallen from his vehicle, resulting in a pedestrian being injured.
It has been noted that the fuel consumption of John's vehicle is significantly higher than similar vehicles in the fleet.
Which of the following options are likely to have caused the partial load loss?
Select TWO of the options below.
Insecure load
Other road user
Poor observation
Excessive speed
Weather conditions
Help
Review Screen
Previous
Next

☐ Select for Review

Case Study

John is the driver of a flatbed LGV and is nearing the end of a nine-hour driving day. He has taken appropriate breaks. As he negotiates a right-hand bend he notices in his mirror that a roll of steel has fallen from his vehicle, resulting in a pedestrian being injured.

It has been noted that the fuel consumption of John's vehicle is significantly higher than similar vehicles in the fleet.

The diagram below shows the original position of the vehicle before the load fell off.

Which direction will the load have travelled?

To answer the question, use your mouse to click directly on the image below.

A red X will mark the place you choose.

To change your answer, click a new place.

☐ Select for Review

Case Study

John is the driver of a flatbed LGV and is nearing the end of a nine-hour driving day. He has taken appropriate breaks. As he negotiates a right-hand bend he notices in his mirror that a roll of steel has fallen from his vehicle, resulting in a pedestrian being injured.

It has been noted that the fuel consumption of John's vehicle is significantly higher than similar vehicles in the fleet.

Who has the legal responsibility for ensuring that the load is secure?

Select the BEST option below.

☐ John

☐ John's employer

☐ John and his employer

☐ Neither John nor his employer

Case Study

John is the driver of a flatbed LGV and is nearing the end of a nine-hour driving day. He has taken appropriate breaks. As he negotiates a right-hand bend he notices in his mirror that a roll of steel has fallen from his vehicle, resulting in a pedestrian being injured.

It has been noted that the fuel consumption of John's vehicle is significantly higher than similar vehicles in the fleet.

Having stopped at the scene of the incident, what is the first action that John should take?

Select the BEST option below.

☐ Call the police

☐ Call his employer

☐ Make the area safe

☐ Give first aid to the injured pedestrian

Case Study

John is the driver of a flatbed LGV and is nearing the end of a nine-hour driving day. He has taken appropriate breaks. As he negotiates a right-hand bend he notices in his mirror that a roll of steel has fallen from his vehicle, resulting in a pedestrian being injured.

It has been noted that the fuel consumption of John's vehicle is significantly higher than similar vehicles in the fleet.

Based on the information in the scenario, what may have affected John's level of concentration immediately prior to the incident?

Select the BEST option below.

☐ Tiredness

☐ Intake of alcohol

☐ Traffic congestion

☐ Weather conditions

⑦ Help ⏩ Review Screen   ← Previous   Next →

What happens next

After you've completed the first case study, the 'Next' button will take you to the next case study, and so on, until you've completed all of them.

You'll be able to go back to double-check (and, if necessary, change) answers in previous case studies at any time until you complete the test.

Your results will be available within 10 minutes of completing the entire test.

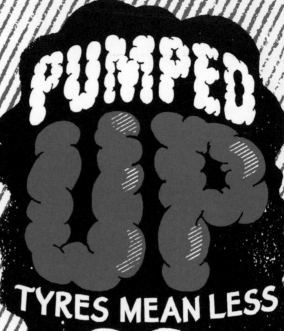

PUMPED UP
TYRES MEAN LESS CO₂

Underinflated tyres mean your engine is working harder. Keeping them at the right pressure burns less fuel and cuts your CO₂ emissions. For more about CO₂, visit www.gov.uk

ACT ON CO₂

section five
THE PRACTICAL DEMONSTRATION TEST

This section covers
- What to expect
- The questions

What to expect

The Driver CPC Practical Demonstration Test (also known as Module 4) has been introduced to allow you to prove that you can carry out a number of operations, other than driving, which are legal requirements. The examiner will expect you to show that you can

- prepare for duty in a safe manner
- ensure that your vehicle is fit for service
- take measures to ensure that illegal immigrants or goods are prevented from being carried
- understand and use safe working practices
- stay aware of certain other aspects of driving practice that cover safety and compliance, and the loading and securing methods that must be used with different types of goods to be carried (for example, bales, metal loads, loose building materials, etc).

The test is interactive and you'll be expected to explain and demonstrate your actions. Thirty minutes is allowed for this test, during which the examiner will ask you to explain and demonstrate how you would deal with certain situations. These situations are described later in this section.

You're expected to provide a vehicle that complies with the minimum test vehicle standards for this module and you'll be asked to demonstrate your knowledge using that vehicle.

In general, vehicles presented for CPC Module 4 tests must meet the same minimum test vehicle specification as applies to the corresponding PCV or LGV licence acquisition practical test. However, vehicles used for Module 4 tests need not have those items that are solely for the use of the examiner during the on-road driving part of the licence acquisition test (eg additional mirrors and a suitable seat from which the test can be conducted).

There are five topic areas, and for each you'll be asked a number of questions. Currently, you're expected to achieve an overall pass mark of 80%, as well as achieving at least 75% in each of the topics. These topic areas are shown overleaf.

The following types of organisation can now apply to DVSA to carry out Driver CPC Module 4 tests for their customers:

- LGV/PCV training organisations
- haulage companies
- bus/coach companies
- LGV/PCV industry training associations
- Driver CPC periodic training centres.

Contact DVSA for further details:

Email technicalstandards@dvsa.gov.uk
Tel 0115 936 6370

The questions

The test will contain questions on each of the following areas.

Demonstrate how to load a vehicle with due regard for safety rules and proper vehicle use

You need to demonstrate

- that you can calculate the weights that contribute to the total weight of a vehicle, and explain what would indicate to you that your vehicle was improperly loaded or overloaded

- how to safely distribute any load that you intend to carry on your vehicle and secure it with the correct restraining device so that it will remain stable on the road.

Show that you know how to secure the vehicle and its contents

You need to demonstrate

- how to secure your vehicle and make every effort to reduce the risk of it being stolen when you park, especially at night

- an understanding of how the braking system works and be able to carry out physical checks to assess correct operation. You should also know what to do if you find a fault

- how to check that all wheels, tyres, spray suppression equipment, etc on your vehicle and any trailer are in a serviceable condition

ENSURE TWISTLOCKS
DISENGAGE BEFORE
LIFTING CONTAINER
DEC00071

- your familiarity with the physical dimensions and clearances required for the vehicle, any restrictions that may apply, and your awareness of any overhangs or projections when driving

- how to check the vehicle controls and gauges as part of your 'cockpit drill' and the action to take when a warning light is showing.

Demonstrate an ability to prevent criminality and trafficking in illegal immigrants

You need to demonstrate

- an awareness of the security of your vehicle and its contents and explain what procedures to adopt when crossing borders, particularly when leaving and returning to the United Kingdom

- where illegal packages or immigrants may be hidden on your vehicle and what checks you as the driver need to make to comply with any cross-border legislation.

Demonstrate an ability to assess emergency situations

You should be able to demonstrate and explain

- the measures you would undertake in extreme weather, especially in regard to diesel fuel and driving visual aids

- the emergency procedure to adopt if your vehicle catches fire during your journey, and be able to identify the various types of fire extinguisher and know which fires they're intended to tackle

- how to enter and exit your vehicle safely with due regard for other road users and pedestrians.

Demonstrate an ability to prevent physical risk

You should be able to demonstrate and explain

- the precautions to take before starting the engine

- the walk-round safety checks you would make on your vehicle before starting each and every journey. This should also include items that need to be checked from inside the vehicle. Use a driver's safety check sheet if you wish.

YOU DRIVE FOR A LIVING BUT YOU'D KILL FOR SOME SLEEP?

Tiredness Kills. Make time for a break.
think.direct.gov.uk

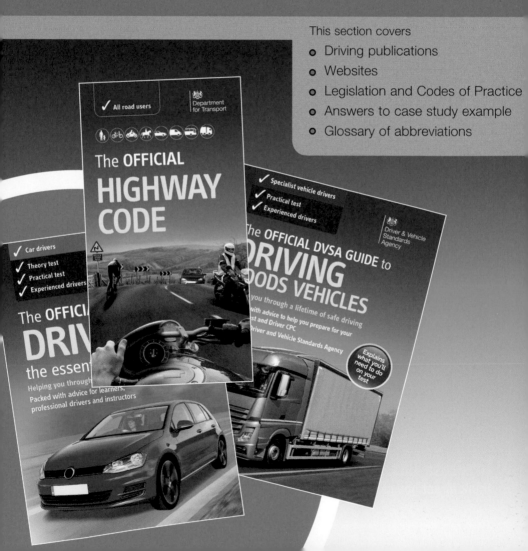

section **six**

FURTHER INFORMATION

This section covers

- Driving publications
- Websites
- Legislation and Codes of Practice
- Answers to case study example
- Glossary of abbreviations

✓ All road users

Department for Transport

The **OFFICIAL**
HIGHWAY
CODE

✓ Specialist vehicle drivers
✓ Practical test
✓ Experienced drivers

Driver & Vehicle Standards Agency

The **OFFICIAL DVSA GUIDE** to
DRIVING
GOODS VEHICLES

...you through a lifetime of safe driving
...with advice to help you prepare for your
...est and Driver CPC
...river and Vehicle Standards Agency

Explains what you'll need to do on your test

✓ Car drivers
✓ Theory test
✓ Practical test
✓ Experienced drivers

The **OFFICIA**
DRIV
the essen

Helping you through
Packed with advice for learners,
professional drivers and instructors

Driving publications

Department for Transport
Know Your Traffic Signs
The Stationery Office, London.
Free PDF download available at **www.gov.uk**

Department for Transport
*Reported Road Casualties Great Britain,
Transport Statistics Great Britain*
Free PDF downloads available at **www.gov.uk**

Department for Transport and Driver and
Vehicle Standards Agency
The Official Highway Code*
The Stationery Office, London.
Available online at **www.gov.uk**

Driver and Vehicle Standards Agency
*Guide to maintaining roadworthiness:
Commercial goods and passenger carrying
vehicles*
Free PDF download available at
www.gov.uk

Driver and Vehicle Standards Agency
*The Official DVSA Guide to Driving –
the essential skills**
The Stationery Office, London.

Driver and Vehicle Standards Agency
*The Official DVSA Theory Test for Drivers
of Large Vehicles**
The Stationery Office, London.

Driver and Vehicle Standards Agency
*The Official DVSA Guide to Driving
Goods Vehicles**
The Stationery Office, London.

Health and Safety Executive
'Health and safety in road haulage' (leaflet)
Free PDF download available at **hse.gov.uk**

Health and Safety Executive
The health and safety toolbox
hse.gov.uk/toolbox

Vehicle and Operator Services Agency
*Heavy Goods Vehicle Inspection Manual
Rules on Drivers' Hours and Tachographs:
Goods vehicles in GB and Europe* (2011)
(VOSA publication GV262)
Free PDF downloads available at
www.gov.uk

Driver and Vehicle Agency (NI)
*Rules on Drivers' Hours and Tachographs:
Goods vehicles in Northern Ireland
and Europe*
Free PDF download available at
doeni.gov.uk

* Please check on
  safedrivingforlife.info/shop that you
  have the most recent version.

Websites

General CPC information
www.gov.uk/topic/transport/driver-cpc

Department for Transport (DfT)
www.gov.uk/dft

Driver and Vehicle Agency (DVA in NI)
nidirect.gov.uk/motoring

Driver and Vehicle Licensing Agency (DVLA)
www.gov.uk/dvla

Freight Transport Association (FTA)
fta.co.uk

Health and Safety Executive (HSE)
hse.gov.uk

Highways England
www.gov.uk/highways

HM Revenue and Customs (HMRC)
www.gov.uk/hmrc

Joint Approvals Unit for Periodic Training (JAUPT)
jaupt.org.uk

Road Haulage Association (RHA)
rha.uk.net

Safe Driving for Life
safedrivingforlife.info

See also
legislation.gov.uk

Advisory, Conciliation and Arbitration Service (Acas)
acas.org.uk

Legislation and Codes of Practice

Legislation

Carriage of Dangerous Goods by Road Regulations 1996.

Carriage of Dangerous Goods Amendments Regulations 1999.

Carriage of Dangerous Goods and Use of Transportable Pressure Equipment Regulations 2009.

Driver CPC EU Directive 2003/59. Official Journal L226/4 10/09/2003.

EU Drivers' Hours Regulations 561/2006. Official Journal L102 11/04/2006 P.1-14.

EU Drivers Hours Regulations 521/2006. Official Journal L093 31/03/2006 P.0043-0044.

Motor Vehicles (Driving Licences) (Amendment) Regulations 2008, SI 2008 No 508.

Motor Vehicles (Driving Licences) (Amendment No. 2) Regulations 2010, SI 2010 No 1203.

Motor Vehicles (Driving Licences) Regulations (Northern Ireland) 1996.

The Road Transport (Working Time) Regulations 2005. SI 2005 No. 639.

The Road Vehicles (Construction and Use) (Amendment) Regulations 2000. SI 2000 No. 1434.

Motor Vehicles (Construction and Use) Regulations (NI) 1999.

Road Traffic Act 1991.

The Transport Act 1968.

Note: UK legislation is available from **legislation.gov.uk** for Acts and Statutory Instruments. Many items are available to view online or can be referenced at your local library.

Codes of Practice

Code of Practice for Safe Use of Cranes. Lorry Loaders (BS7121-4). British Standards Institute.

Lorry Loaders: The Code of Practice for Installation, Application and Operation. ALLMI.

Roll-on, Roll-off Ships: Stowage and Securing of Vehicles – Code of Practice. DfT Marine Directorate.

Merchant Shipping Notice M1445 or BSEN 29367. Department for Trade.

Code of Practice for the Selection and Care of Tyres and Wheels for Commercial Vehicles. British Standards Institute.

Answers to case study example

Category	Answer
Case Study – John	
Question 1 (page 65)	Insecure load Excessive speed
Question 2 (page 66)	Left rear corner of the vehicle
Question 3 (page 67)	John
Question 4 (page 68)	Make the area safe
Question 5 (page 69)	Tiredness

Glossary of abbreviations

Acas – Advisory, Conciliation and Arbitration Service

ALLMI – Association of Lorry Loader Manufacturers and Importers of Great Britain

BSI – British Standards Institute

CMR – Convention on the Contract for the International Carriage of Goods by Road

CPC – Certificate of Professional Competence (for Drivers)

DfT – Department for Transport

DQC – Driver Qualification Card

DVA – Driver and Vehicle Agency (Northern Ireland)

DVLA – Driver and Vehicle Licensing Agency

DVSA – Driver and Vehicle Standards Agency

EC – European Community

EU – European Union

GB – Great Britain

GPS – Global Positioning System

GVW – gross vehicle weight

HSE – Health and Safety Executive

ISO – International Standards Organisation

JAUPT – Joint Approvals Unit for Periodic Training

LGV – large goods vehicle

MAM – maximum authorised mass

MPW – maximum permissible weight

MTV – minimum test vehicle

NI – Northern Ireland

NVQ – National Vocational Qualification

PCV – passenger-carrying vehicle

SAFED – safe and fuel-efficient driving

SSC – Sector Skills Council

SVQ – Scottish Vocational Qualification

TIR – Transports Internationaux Routiers (International Road Transport)

UK – United Kingdom

VDU – visual display unit

VIN – Vehicle Identification Number

WTD – Working Time Directive

Learning to drive, ride or simply want to brush up on your knowledge?

- All the latest revision questions and answers
- Over 100 high-quality hazard perception clips
- Accessible on any internet-connected device

Visit **www.dvsalearningzone.co.uk** and enter code **SD10** to save 10%.